Ralph Ayres' Cookery Book

Ralph Ayres' Cookery Book

With an Introduction and Glossary
by Jane Jakeman

BODLEIAN LIBRARY · UNIVERSITY OF OXFORD

Editorial note

The letters 'u' and 'v' in this manuscript of the cookery book have been regularized in the transcription in accordance with modern spelling. However, capitalization has been retained as it seems in the manuscript.

First published in 2006 by the Bodleian Library
Broad Street
Oxford OX1 3BG

www.bodleianbookshop.co.uk

ISBN 1 85124 075 6

Designed by Dot Little. Cover design by Jessica Harvey
Printed and bound by sellier druck GmbH, Freising, Germany
British Library Catalogue in Publishing Data
A CIP record of this publication is available from the British Library

Manuscript pages from *Ralph Ayres Cookery Book* are reproduced from Bodleian Library, MS. Don.e.89.

Botanical illustrations are from *Phytanthoza iconographia, sive, Conspectus aliquot millium*, 8 vols., published by Johann Wilhelm Weinmann (Regensburg, 1737-1745), Arch.Nat. hist. G 5-12.

Contents

Foreword

This small book of handwritten recipes bears on its titlepage the inscription 'Radolphus Ayres Cook Oxford 1721'. It was given to the Bodleian Library in 1959 by the Friends of the Bodleian who bought it from P. L. H. Smith.

In its day it may have been a popular little book in Oxford, for two other copies are known. One was edited in 1922 by L.G. Wickham Legg and printed for private circulation under the title *A little book of recipes of New College two hundred years ago*. On the verso of its first leaf was the inscription 'Radolphus Ayres Cook of Newcolidg in Oxford 1721'. The present whereabouts of this copy is not known. Another copy is in the archives of New College, Oxford (reference no. 962), and bears the title 'Radolphus Ayres Cook of New Collidg in Oxford 1719', but has no ownership inscription earlier than 1861. All the three manuscripts appear to have been bound in a flowery patterned paper over thin pasteboard; and all were copied in a similar way, with Ralph Ayres' recipes on the recto of each leaf, and the verso left blank for subsequent additions. Only the Bodleian copy lacks additions of this kind.

The collection of recipes is substantially the same in all three manuscripts: the recipes occur in the same order, and two manuscripts (those from Bodley and from New College) are probably in the same handwriting. Yet there are one or two odd and apparently inexplicable differences. In place of the two veal dishes on folio 35 of our manuscript, which occur on folio 32 of the New College manuscript, Legg's manuscript has recipes for preserving lemons and oranges. The recipe 'to pott a Haire', on folio 21 of our manuscript and folio 22 of Legg's manuscript, is replaced in the New College manuscript by a recipe 'To Make a Tanzy'. The New College manuscript lacks the recipe 'To make a Cabage Puding' (Bodley manuscript, folio 28; Legg's manuscript folio 29); nor does it have the 'Rich Seed Cake' recipe (Bodley, folio 30; Legg, folio 31). The 'Jelly of Rasberyes' (Bodley, folio 29; Legg, folio 30) is also missing and the 'Jam of Rasberyes' (Bodley, folio 27; Legg, folio 28) is replaced by 'a marmalad of cherries' in the New College manuscript. In the Bodley manuscript page 31 has been left blank, and so is not reproduced in this book.

Whatever the reason for these differences, what we have is a group of three recipe books, all apparently originating from a Ralph Ayres, who was cook at New College, Oxford, in the first quarter of the eighteenth century. It is not possible to say whether any of them actually belonged to Ayres, and the early history of the Bodleian manuscript is not known. The scribbled names of Catherine (folio 20) and Elizabeth (folio 16) are our only apparent clues.

Ralph Ayres himself is a shadowy figure. The registers of St Mary Magdalen parish record the burial of a Ralph Ayres in November 1741, and an inscription in the church gives his age as 40. But this would mean he was only 19 at the time of the compilation of the earliest recipe book, and in any case the parish register describes him as 'musician'. It is more likely that the recipes are the work of Ralph Ayres of the parish of St Peter in the east, who was probably the father of the musician mentioned above. The earlier Ralph Ayres is described as a wheelwright in the record of his marriage at St Cross Church in 1691, but we can only assume that during the next twenty-five years he developed an interest in cooking. We are left in the position of knowing far more about the recipes than we can discover about the cook.

The recipes themselves contain one or two dishes of local interest. Oxford sausages (folio 2) are not called 'Oxford' in the earliest manuscript, but this mixture of veal and pork has been a well-known Oxford product for centuries. Ayres himself is credited with the pancakes on folio 20 and the pudding on folio 30, and New College puddings (for which there is a recipe on folio 19) are also found in many subsequent recipe books.

The first comment of the modern cook on these recipes will inevitably refer to their richness and indigestibility. Modern theories of diet do not commend such mixtures of brandy, ale, sherry, sugar, butter, eggs and cream.

The methods of cooking available in the eighteenth century were limited: food could be boiled or stewed, or cooked slowly in the oven. However, the most striking differences are concerned with the preservation of food. Refrigeration has made obsolete the elaborate procedures described here for preserving, pickling, and bottling which were the only methods of storing food. Nor do we need to resort to so many highly spiced flavourings in order to make preserved foods palatable.

Quantities in Ralph Ayres' recipes tend to be vague. The recipe for 'Custards' specifies only that the cook should 'put in what quantity of fine shugar you see good', so the recipes were not intended for cooks.

But whether you choose to try out the recipes or not, Ralph Ayres' little book remains an evocative reminder of the gargantuan appetites of our ancestors.

David Vaisey
Bodley's Librarian Emeritus

Introduction

When the Reverend James Woodforde, Fellow of New College, entertained a party of friends to a private dinnner in the College on July 27, 1774, he noted in his diary that the meal included green pea soup, mutton, a goose, peas, and an apple tart with cream, followed by a handsome dish of fruit. The meal was washed down with beer, cider and ales, and port and madeira were served afterwards. Prominent on the menu was New College Pudding.

The composition of this dinner had probably not changed in the thirty years or so since the days when Ralph ('Radolphus' as he was dignified in Latin) Ayres, author of this little recipe book, ruled the New College kitchen, and the reader will find in these pages the recipe for those hefty delights, the celebrated College Pudding and Quaking Pudding which accompanied it.

David Vaisey's Foreword to this edition supplies bibliographical information about the manuscript versions of Ayres' book and the scanty biographical information available. Ayres was a popular name in Oxfordshire and Ralph's family cannot be identified with any certainty. A family called Ayres was in the butchery trade in Hook Norton at the end of the seventeenth century, and one Bernett Ayres is recorded as an inn-holder in the same village (which still has a celebrated brewery) in 1698.[1] Certainly, the background of an inn-keeper's son would have provided good training for the large-scale catering needed for a college.

In Ayres' time, New College itself retained many of the traditions, and indeed the buildings, of its founder, William of Wykeham, Bishop of Winchester and Chancellor of England, who had founded the institution in 1379 with a warden and seventy 'scholars', or Fellows. Its purpose was to continue the education of the boys educated at the school he had founded at Winchester. He required the Fellows to live in a very modest style, a tradition which was happily not maintained in later centuries: on Shrove Tuesday, 1775, to mark the beginning of the Lenten Fast, it is recorded that the Fellows were served with lobsters, pancakes and plum cake, on which the college butler had placed 'a copy of verses of his own making'.[2]

The eighteenth-century New College cooks inherited a great medieval kitchen with its timber roof, where the main means of cooking would have originally been in cauldrons or on spits or jacks before an open fire, the smoke issuing from an opening above. The kitchen was in a separate block outside the main quadrangle which reduced the fire risk to the rest of the buildings.

In the sixteenth century, some improvements had been installed when the open hearth was replaced by two large fireplaces with a chimney. The spits were still in use in Ayres' time, for spit-roasting remained a preferred means of cooking in England throughout the eighteenth century: it gave a more regular and reliable heat than unpredictable ovens.

A cook like Ayres would have had a number of complicated spit-roasting mechanisms available. Some repairs must have taken place, for Thomas Hearne, an Oxford diarist, noted in January, 1727, 'the wind being extraordinarily high (and it being a strange dismal Wet day) in the forenoon the Kitchen Chimney of New College fell down, and broke the Ribs of the man that turned the Spit (but 'tis hoped he may be recovered) and spoiled all the meat and the Fire. It was a very odd, rotten old chimney.'[3]

The kitchen had a considerable degree of self-reliance: it had bread-ovens as well as the open fires, and the College had a pigeon-loft, possessed its own well, brewed its own beer, and grew much of its vegetable produce. The sense of community was accentuated by all the members having attended the same school. It was thus a homogenous group for whom the chef had to cater—men of much the same background and tastes. This was not a time of any great intellectual activity in Oxford, and since it was not necessary to take an examination to gain a degree there was no great compulsion to learn or to teach; it was, however, a period of great sociability, with the development of common rooms within the colleges and coffee houses outside them, and the pleasures of living were generally appreciated.

A number of people must have been employed in the business of cooking and the scene when Ayres was in charge probably resembled that in an engraving of the kitchen at Christ Church,[4] a hive of frantic activity and billowing smoke where men and women are preparing food at trestle tables and attending to roasts. In addition, the Warden had his own kitchen, and he and other members of the College, like the diarist Woodforde, could order private feasts for themselves and their guests. The commissariat of such an enterprise was therefore a considerable business.

The role of head cook would have had something in common with catering for one of the London clubs or guilds, where the demands of a community had to be reconciled with personal tastes. This 'collegiate cuisine' has certain characteristics which we can observe also in the early eighteenth-century recipe book of Edward Kidder,[5] who probably had a large clientèle in the City of London serving such institutions as the London Companies and Guilds. It is masculine, meaty, strong on filling substances such as pastry and puddings, and caters generously for those with a sweet tooth. The quantities are large and the recipes include dishes which can be served with a flourish, such as the elaborate instructions for presenting veal olives on spits set around a roast fowl with the optional additions of forcemeat balls, sausages, oysters, and mushrooms.

The recipes have much traditional content, for example the instructions for adding anchovies to a gravy, something unusual in modern cookery, but which has a long culinary history, probably going back to the garum or salty fish-based sauce which was a basic of Roman cookery. Another traditional condiment found in Ayres' book is varjuice, or verjuice, an acid liquor obtained from unripe fruit (p. 15). Verjuice is found in medieval recipes, and indeed also in the Roman cookery book of Apicius. Medieval chefs also served up 'mince pies' containing meat, with the combination of sweet and savoury flavours which has always been a feature of British tastes. And we find such indications of long-standing practices as the recipe for fricassée of rabbit or chicken, by which Ayres means a thick brown stew rather than the more delicate and modern white sauce dish.

Some recipes are more familiar: that for Queen Cakes, for example, still a favourite, and the lemon and orange tarts which in the next century were perhaps an inspiration for Alice in Wonderland. The New College chef still occasionally prepares the famous Pudding. The most striking evidence of contemporaneity is undoubtedly Ayres' generous quantities of sugar, which in the first half of the eighteenth century became cheap and plentiful in Britain as the result of the exploitation of slave labour in the West Indies. It has been estimated that British consumption of sugar quadrupled between 1700 and 1740,[6] though in 1751 a tax did something to reduce its lavish use. The large quantities consumed reflect its virtue as a preservative, not just as a sweetener.

In comparison with such recipe books as that of Hannah Glasse, first published in 1747, which were designed for the new gentry in the middle-class home, Ayres is notably lacking in dainty dishes or household hints. In this respect, the copy given here is a primal version, for the others have had domestic additions noted on their pages. The other manuscript in the Bodleian (MS. Don. e.131) presumably passed at some stage in the eighteenth century into female hands. It contains a recipe for treating sore nipples which must have made the patient look like a cross between Salome and a Christmas turkey.[7]

The manuscript, printed in 1922 also has evidence of household usage, with additions by later hands. These include medical hints such as how to deal with the bite of a mad dog or Mr. Dick's 'infallible' honey and lemon cough mixture (the poppy elixir listed among the ingredients would have been an opiate), and also advice on decorative elements such as the candying of angelica. In that 1922 edition, the foreword by L. G. Wickham Legg records a tradition that the manuscript had been shown to Mrs Glasse, who gave the 'New College Pudding' recipe, scaled down appropriately, under the heading, 'An Oxford Pudding' in her book. However, Wickam Legg concluded that 'Mrs Glasse herself did not form a favourable opinion of our college cooking in the time of Queen Anne.'[8]

It was a cuisine appropriate to the community it served, one which still conducted itself with some formality. College breakfast, however, was nothing like the 'English breakfast' of today. It consisted of some light snack such as hot rolls and tea or chocolate, supplied, not in Hall, but carried from the College Buttery, which, then as now, served snack-type food, to individual rooms for private consumption. Dinner, usually served in Oxford between midday and 2 pm in the mid-eighteenth century, was the main meal of the day, at which dons were expected to wear white waistcoats, wigs and gowns. Until 1830, New College had a special tradition whereby two choristers proceeded from the gateway to the dining hall singing out in a mongrel of Latin and French, 'Tempus vocandi à manger O seigneurs!' ('Time to call you to dine, my masters!'). There would, of course, be a formal grace before the meal began. Food was served in two main courses, and sweet and savoury dishes were mixed. At a dinner in 1774 the first course included cod with oysters, ham, fowls, boiled beef, rabbits smothered with onions, mutton, veal collops, pork griskins (lean part of the loin), New College Puddings, Mince Pies and roots (vegetables). In the second course were roast turkey, haunch of venison, a brace of woodcocks, snipes, veal olives, trifle, blancmange, stewed pippins and preserved quinces.[9]

High Table, the raised dais where the dons dined, would be adorned for special feasts with the college plate, which at New College included some splendid salt-cellars and a number of elaborate drinking-vessels—some made from coconuts—and an array of handsome silver tankards which had been donated by various past members. During the time of Ralph Ayres the New College bursars ordered such things as tankards and sauce-boats to be fashioned out of existing worn or outmoded silver vessels. Wine, varying with the wealth of the college and the foresight of its purchasers, accompanied dinner. The main meal was followed by cheese, fruit, port, and any toasts or celebrations appropriate to the season. Supper, a meal often made up of cold meats and taken in private quarters, was served at about six o'clock, so there might be only a short interval between meals. At supper, potted and salted meats, important recipes in Ayres' book, would have been consumed. The day might be rounded off with a snack, perhaps a hot pie or some small cakes, served with punch, an egg-flip or a negus of spiced wine and lemon, and at last the weary cooks could repose. Until breakfast, of course!

Jane Jakeman, Oxford, 2005

[2] Oxfordshire Probate Records, 1516-1732, p. 23, 107.232, 160/1/34. I am indebted for this reference to Mrs Caroline Dalton, the New College archivist.

[3] Graham Midgley, *University Life in Eighteenth-Century Oxford* (New Haven and London: Yale University Press, 1996), p. 43.

[4] *The Remains of Thomas Hearne*, ed. John Buchanan-Brown (London: Centaur Press, 1966), p. 326.

[5] Bodleian Library, Oxford, Dept. of Printed Books, G.A.Oxon. h. 109 b.p. 76.

[6] *Kidder's Receipts: an eighteenth century recipe book*, with an introduction by Jane Jakeman (Oxford: Ashmolean Museum, 2001).

[7] Sidney W. Mintz, *Sweetness and power, the place of sugar in modern history* (Harmondsworth: Penguin, 1985), p. 67.

[8] 'A penneworth of Litherige of Gold [monoxide of red lead] mixt with Vinegar then put sweet oil to make it like an ointment. Beat together for two hours. Anoint ye Niples with a feather then put on Green Sage leaves Round em' (fol. IV) The sage may have had some healing properties.

[9] *A Little Book of Recipes of New College two hundred years ago* (Oxford: Oxford University Press, 1922), p. 2.

[10] Graham Midgley, *University Life in Eighteenth Century Oxford* (New Haven and London: Yale University Press, 1996) p. 42.

To make a plain Cake (1)

take 4 pound of flour 3 pound of Currans, one pound of
Raisins stoned & Chopped small, then take 2 nutmegs
& make y.e one ounce with mace & Cincmon beat
fine, & so Cloues one pound of suger, & mixe these
well together, then take a pint of aleyest, 10 Eggs &
leaue out 5 whites, then beat the Eggs & yest well
togather with 4 spoonfulls of the best brandy, & strain
it in the midle of the flour, then pour in of one
side a pint & a half of Cream with one pound
of butter mellted theirin pour it in when luke
warme, & mix it well togather, with Candied orang
Lemmon & Cittorn each 2 ounces, & let it stand one
hour by the fire to rise before you put it in
the hoop, & bake it 3 hours or longer ———

To make the Ice for the Cake

beat the whites of 3 Eggs with 3 Quarters of a
pound of Double refined suger sifted beat it for
half an hour or longer, so the Cake being baked lay
on the Ice & harden it att the ouins mouth —

To make a plum Cake

take 4 pound of flour, 3 pound of Currans, one pound of raisins
stoned & Chopped small, then take 2 nuttmeg & make y^m
one ounce with mace & Cinemon beat fine, & 30 Cloves one
pound of suger, & mix these well togather, then take a pint
of aleyest, 10 Eggs & Leaue out 5 whites, then beat the Eggs
& yest well togather with 4 spoonfulls of the best brandy, &
Strain it in the midle of the flour, then pour in of one side
a pint & a half of Cream with one pound of butter mellted
theirin pour it in when luke warme & mix it well togather with
Candied orang Lemmon & Cittorn Each 2 ounces & let it
stand one hour by the fire to rise befor you put it in the hoop
& bake it 3 hours or longer

To make the Ice for the Cake

beat the whites of 3 Eggs with 3 quarters of a pound of
Doublerefined suger sifted beat it for half an hour or longer, So
the Cake being baked lay on the Ice & harden it att the ovins
mouth

(2)

To make bath Cakes, to serue in the wine Coffee or tea

take one pound of the finest flour, & rubb fine
in it allmost half a pound of butter, half a
pound of fine suger, half an ounce of Carrawayseds
4 spoonfulls of the best brandy and as much sack
& what roase watter will temper it in a paist,
then make them in little thin round Cakes & wash
them ouer with roasewatter, & scrape ouer some
Doublrefined suger; & bake them on tinn — —

To make Oxford Sausages

take of poark & ueal an Eaqull Quantity, & let it
be free from sinnes & skin & Chop it very small,
then add to it half as much good beef suet as meat
& Chopp it togather till the suet is fine, then
season it with pepper salt nuttmeg, some sage
& thyme minced small, then worke it up
with 2 or 3 Eggs & a little watter as you se good

To make bath Cakes, sarve y^m wth wine Coffee or tea

take one pound of the finest flour, & rubb fine in it allmost half a pound of butter, half a pound of fine suger, half an ounce of Carraway seeds, 4 spoonfulls of the best brandy and as much sack & what roase watter will temper it in a paist, then make them in little thin round cakes & wash them over with roase watter, & scrape over some Doublerefined suger, & bake them on tinn

To make Oxford Sausages

take of poark & veal an Eaqull Quantity, & let it be free from Sinues & Skin & Chop it very small, then add to it half as much good beef suet as meat and Chopp it togather till the suet is fine, then season it with pepper salt nuttmeg, some sage & thyme minced small, then worke it up with 2 or 3 Eggs & a little watter as you see good

(3)

To make naples Bisket

beat 8 Eggs in a larg bowl or pan with 3 spoonfulls of roase watter, then whipp $\overset{m}{y}$ to a light froth, strewing ᵉ in all the same time one pound of $\overset{e}{y}$ finest powder suger sifted, then take out the whisk & sift in one pound of the finest flour, & then mix it well togather so your pans being papord fill them & scrape over some Doublerefined suger & bake them that minuit if possable —

To make Bisket Dropps

take 3 large Eggs & leave out one white, 2 spoonfulls of roase watter, half a pound of singlerefined suger, sifted a few Carrawayseeds then whipp these well togather till it is to a light froth, then take out the whisk & sift in half a pound of the finest flour, & mix it well togather, then Drop them small & Ice them with a little Doublerefined suger & bake $\overset{m}{y}$ as soon as possable

To make naples Bisket

beat 8 Eggs in a larg bowl or pan with 3 spoonfulls of roase watter, then whipp y^m to a light froth, strewing in att the same time one pound of y^e finest powder suger sifted, then take out the whisk & sift in one pound of the finest flour, & then mix it well togather so your pans being papord fill them & scrape over some Doublerefined suger & bake them that minuit if possable

To make Bisket Dropps

take 3 large Eggs & leave out one white, 2 spoonfulls of roase watter, half a pound of singlerefined suger, sifted a few Carraway seeds then whipp these well togather till it is to a light froth, then take out the whisk & sift in half a pound of the finest flour, & mix it well togather, then Drop them small & Ice them with a little Doublerefined suger & bake y^m as soon as possable

To make a (4) Jelly of Pippins

pair & Quarter a Dozen of large pippins &
put them in to a skillat th it is watter will
Just Couer them, then boyl them till they are
very tender then strain of the liquer which
must be no more then about a pint & add
to it one pound of Double refined suger, & y
Juice of 2 Limmons & boyl it till you think
it will gelly keeping it skiming, then strain
it through a mufling bagg in Glasses.——

To make a Jelly of Currance

take one pound of Doublerefined suger, in
powder, & put it in to a skillat with what
watter will wett it or more, so boyl it up &
Clarrefie it with the whik of an Eggs &
skim it Clean of, then put in the Juice of
one Quart of Currance & boyl it till you
think it will Jelly then strain it through a
mufling bagg in Glasses.

To make a Jelly of Pippins

pair & quarter a Dozen of large pippins & put them
into a skillat wth w^t watter will just cover them, then boyl
them till they are very tendar then strain of the liquer which
must be no more than about a pint & add to it one pound
of Doublerefined suger & ye juice of 2 Lemmons & boyl it
till you think it will jelly keeping it skiming, then strain it
through a musling bagg in Glasses

To make a Jelly of Currance

take one pound of Doublerefined suger, in powder, & put it
in to a skillat with what watter will wet it or more, so boyl it
up & Clarreyfie it with the white of an Egg & skim it Clean
of, then put in the juice of one quart of Currance & boyl it till
you think it will jelly then strain it through a musling bagg in
Glasses

(5)   winter

To Keep kidney beans to boyl green all y

take y midle size beans & throw them in boyling
watter with a good handfull of salt, & let them
be in a bout one minuit, then Immaditley take
them out & Dry them on a Cloth & the mean
time put in to that watter a good Deal more salt
to make a strong bryne, of it, so boyl it up &
pour it in to a Deep Earthen pot, & when it
is Cold put in your beans, & pour a Cake
of mutton fat ouer them, & when you boyl
y to Eat pick them & throw them in boyling
watter 3 or 4 hours first & pout in the boyling
a Quarter of a pound of butter. ————

To make Custards

Slice half a nutmeg in a Quart of Cream, & boyle
it & when the rash heat is of put in 10 Eggs
well beat with a little sack or Brandy, &
Leaue out 5 whites, put in a little salt,
& what suger you see good so strain it of &
fill your Custards boyl in the Cream one penney
worth of whole mace & 8 or 10 Cloues

To Keep kidney beans to boyle green all ye winter

take ye midle size beans & throw them in boyling watter with a good handfull of salt, & let them be in a bout one minuit, then Immaditley take them out & Dry them on a cloth & the mean time put in to that watter a good Deal more salt to make a strong bryne, of it, so boyle it up & pour it in to a Deep Earthen pot, & when it is Cold put in your beans, & pour a Cake of mutton fat over them, & when you boyl y^m to Eat pick them & throw them in watter 3 or 4 hours first & put in the boyling a quarter of a pound of butter

To make Custards

Slice half a nuttmeg in a quart of Cream, & boyle it & when the rash heat is of put in 10 Eggs well beat with a little sack or brandey, & Leave out 5 whites, put in a little salt, & what suger you see good so strain it of & fill your Custards boyl in the cream one penney worth of whole mace & 8 or 10 Cloves

To make a (6) Lemmon puding or flur antine

boyl the rids of 2 lemons very kindar in 2 or 3
watters, then beat it fine in a morter with
the meat of the Lemmons picked Clean from
the skin & kernills, then add to it 3 Quarters of
a pound of loaf sueger sifted, 4 grated biskets
the yolks of 10 Eggs beat with a little sack or
brandey, then put in half a pound of Clar
reyfied butter & keep it stirring all one way
till it is Cold then you may put in one ounce
of Candied Lemmon, & as much Cittorn if you
please, to you Dish being garnished wth puffpaist
put in your puding & Cut out a flurantine
pattorn for the lidd,

To make an orang puding

9t is Done the same way as the lemmon
puding but the must be the right sivel orangs
for this use

To make a Lemon puding or flurantine

boyl the ri[n]ds of 2 lemons very tendar in 2 or 3 watters, then beat it fine in a morter with the meat of the Lemmons picked Clean from the skin & kernills, then add to it 3 quarters of a pound of loafe sueger sifted, 4 grated biskets the yolks of 10 Eggs beat with a little sack or brandey, then put in half a pound of Clarreyfied butter & keep it stirring all one way till it is Cold, then you may put in one ounce of Candied Lemmons & as much Cittorn if you please, so your Dish being garnished wth puffpaist put in your puding & Cut out a flurantine pattorn for the lidd

To make an orang puding

It is Done the same way as the lemmon puding but the must be the right sivel orangs for this use

To Pickle Pigeons (7)

First bone them Leaving the legs to the flesh
y being inside out, season it with a little
pepper, salt nuttmeg Lemmonpile & thyme
minced small then a Quarter of anchovies in
Every one, Chopped small, then turn them again
& tye them up att Each hand. then boyl them
tendar in the same sort of pickle as for Collerd
Eells, adding some whole pepper, you may put
in a little white wine if you please, & keep
them in the same pickle —

To Pickle Wallnutts

Gather them when they are about the bigness of a
pigeons Egg or before they have any shell, & put
them in to watter & salt, shifting fresh Every Day
or 2 till you find the bitterness well out, then rub
them Clean & Dry & put them in to the best white
wine vinager whole pepper, some mace & a little
salt, y pour some oyle over them & tye them Down —

To Pickle Pigeons

first bone them Leaving the legs to the flesh y^n ye being in side out, season y^m with a little pepper, salt nuttmeg Lemmonpile & thyme minced small then a quarter of anchovey in Every one, Chopped small, then turn them again & tye them up at Each Eand, then boyl them tendar in the same sort of pickle as for Collord Eells, adding some whole pepper, you may put in a little white wine if you please, & keep them in the same pickle

To Pickle Wallnutts

Gather them when they are a bout the bigness of a pigeons Egge or befor they have any shell, & put them in to watter and salt, shifting fresh Every Day or 2 till you find the bitterness well out, then rub them Clean & Dry & put them in to the best white wine vinager whole pepper, some mace & a little salt, y^n pour some oyle over them & tye them Down

(8)

To make a Rice puding or flurantine

Boyl half a pound of rice very tendar in milk & let
it be thick, & when it is Cold add to it 3 Quarters of a
pound of butter, broke in bitts, or as much good beef
fuet or marrow shrad fine, which you pleafe, put
to it 3 Quarters of a pound of Currans, some nutm,
eg, a little falt, 3 grated byskets or as much bread 5 Eggs
beat with a little sack or Brandey, half a pound
of fine fugar, you may put in one ounce of
Candied Lemmon & as much Cittorn if you
pleafe, then bake it in puffpaist as you Do the
Lemon or orang puding,

To Pott Pigeons or Partridges

first trußs them as for a pye & feafon them with
pepper falt nuttmeg, then bake them tendar in buter,
allow to a Dozen 3 pound, & take them out & let the
Graney run Clean from them, then place them
in another pot more proper, & pour as much
of the butter to them as will Cover y[m] leaning back
the fetling

To make a Rice puding or flurantine

boyl half a pound of rice very tendar in milk & let it be
thick, & when it is Cold add to it 3 quarters of a pound of
butter, broke in bitts, or as much good beef suet or marrow
shrad fine, which you please, put to it 3 quarters of a pound
of Currans, some nuttmeg, a little salt, 3 grated biskets
or as much bread 5 Eggs beat with a little sack or brandey,
half a pound of fine suger, you may put in one ounce of
Candied Lemmon & as much Cittorn if you please, then
bake it in puffpaist as you Do the Lemon or orang puding

To Pot Pigeons or Partridges

First truss them as for a pye & season them with pepper salt
nuttmeg, then bake them tendar in buter allow to a Dozen 3
pound & take out the pot & let the Gravey run Clean from
them, then place them in another pot more proper, & pour as
much of the butter to them as will Cover y^m leaving back the
setlins

To make a Puding for a hare Roasted. (9)

take the liue raw and apple & a bitt of onion
& Chopp it very small, then season it with
peppor salt nuttmeg some Lemmonpile & thyme
minced small, put to it a Quarter of a pound
of butter, & what graked bread will temper it
in a paist, then put it in to the belly of the
hare & sowe it up Cloase, so when the hare
is roasted haue redy 3 Quarters of a pound
of melled butter some good grauey, a little
Clarret, 2 anchoueys so take out the puding &
Dissolue it in the sauce & pour it all ouer
the hair & lay round some barberyes ———

To Pickle Barberyes

Gathor ym when they are full ripe & put them
in to a strong bryne of watter & salt, & pour
a Cake of mutton satt ouer ym & tye ym Down

To make a Puding for a hare Roasted

take the live[r] raw and apple & a bitt of onion & Chopp
it very small, then season it with pepper salt nuttmeg some
Lemmonpile & thyme minced small, put to it a quarter of a
pound of butter, & what grated bread will temper it in a paist,
then put it in to the belly of the hare & sowe it up Cloase, So
when the hare is roasted have redy 3 quarters of a pound of
mellted butter some good gravey, a little Clarret, 2 anchoueys
so take out the puding & Dissolve it in the sauce & pour it all
over the hair & lay round some barberyes

To Pickle Barberyes

Gather y^m when they are full ripe & put them in to a strong
bryne of watter & salt, & pour a Cake of mutton fat over y^m &
tye y^m Down

To Pott (10) Beef or Venison

let it be of the buttock, & to 6 pound salt it with
2 ounces of salt petter, & a good Deal of Common
salt, & let it lye in salt 6 or 8 Dayes, then
Couer it with watter & bake it tender, then pick
out all the skin & fatt, then beat the meat
some time in a Cloth with a rouling pin to
Drink up the watter. then beat it fine in a
morter, & season it will be a bout half an ounce
of pepper & half a large nuttmeg, then pour
to it as much Clarreyfied butter as will temper it in a paist, so press it Cloase in your pot
& pour some butter ouer it, a bout 2 pound
of butter will Do this quantity of beef leauing
back the settins

To Pickle Cloues

they being full blown pull of y green budd &
put the flower in white win Zinager, & some
Loafe suger just to make it of a sweet sower &
tye them Down

To Pott Beef or Venison

let it be of the buttock, & to 6 pound salt it with 2 ounces of salt petter, & a good Deal of Common salt, & let it lye in salt 6 or 8 Dayes, then Cover it with watter & bake it tender, then pick out all the skin & fatt, then beat the meat some time in a Cloth with a rouling pin to Drink up the watter, then beat it fine in a morter, & season it with a bout half an ounce of pepper & half a large nuttmeg, then pour to it as much Clarreyfied butter as will temper it in a paist, so press it Cloase in your pot & pour some butter ouer it, a bout 2 pound of butter will Do this quantity of beef leaving back the setlins

To Pickle Cloues

they being full blown pull of y^e green hudd & put the flower in white win Vinager & some loafe suger just to make it of a sweet sower & tye them Down

To Coller Beef

Let it be of the midle rand skin it & bone it
& salt it as you Do the Poted beef, & let it lye
as long in salt, then season it with pepper,
nuttmeg, some thyme & a little roasemary
minced small, then roul it up in a Coller
& bind it hard up with coars tape, then bake
it tendar in watter as you Do the poted beef,
then take of the tape & roul the Coller up in
a Cloth & tye the Cloth att each end then bind y
tape prettey hard all round on the Cloth & to close
the Coller & when it is Cold take of the Cloth
& then you may Cut it when you please. —

To make good puffpast for flurantins or tartlits

allow to a pound of flour 3 quarters of a
pound of butter, & 3 Eggs, Devide the butter
in 4 parts break in one & roul in the rest
att 3 times

To Coller Beef

Let it be of the midle rand skin it & bone it & salt it as you
Do the Poted beef, and let it lye as long in salt, then season it
with pepper, nuttmeg, some thyme & a little roasemary minced
small, then roul it up in a Coller & bind it hard up with Coars
tape, then bake it tendar in watter as you Do the poted beef,
then take of the tape & roul the Coller up in a Cloth and tye
the Cloth att Each end then bind y^e tape prettey hard all round
on the Cloth to Cloas the Coller & when it is Cold take of the
Cloth & then you may Cut it when you please

To make good puffpast for flurantins or tartlits

allow to a pound of flour 3 quarters of a pound of butter, & 3
Eggs, Devide the butter in 4 parts brak in one & roul in the
rest att 3 times

To Coller Eells

(12)

they being Scowrd & Dryd in a Cloth Split y͘
up the back & take out the gutts & the
back bone Cut of the head & taile, & wash y͘
Eells Clean & Dry them on a Cloth & season
them with pepper salt nuttmeg, a little whole
mace broke in bitts & some Lemmon pile & thyme
minced small, then roul them up in Collers
& bind them hard up with Coars tape, then
boyl them tendar in watter some vinager
some salt & a sprigg of thyme then take y͘m
out & pour of the pickle & when it is cold put
in your Collers.

To Pott Eells

Stripp y͘m & gut y͘m & scotch them with a knife &
season y͘m as you do to Coller, then truss them round
& Do them in butter as you Do y͘ poted pigeous.

To Coller Eells

they being scowrd & Dryd in a Cloth splitt y^m up the back & take out the gutts & the back bone Cut of the head & taile & wash the Eells Clean & Dry them on a Cloth & season them with pepper salt nuttmeg, a little whole mace broke in bitts & some Lemmonpile & thyme minced small, then roul them up in Collers & bind them hard up with Coars tape, then boyl them tendar in watter some vinager some salt & a sprigg of thyme then take y^m out & pour of the pickle & when it is Cold put in y^our Collers

To Pott Eells

Stripp y^m and gut y^m & Scotch them with a knife & season y^m as you Do to Coller, them truss them round & Do them in butter as you Do y^e poted pigeons

To make a (13) Dish of Scotch Collops

take a Large fillet of Veal & cut of all the skin,
then Cut the Veal out in large thin Collops, &
hack them with the back of a Large knife, &
season them with salt nuttmeg some Lemmonpi=
le & thyme minced small, put on the yolks of
2 or 3 Eggs & mix them all up togather, &
fry them in butter as white as you Can, then
pour out all most all the Liquer & put in
half a pint of good beef grauey, a Quarter of a
pint of white wine 2 anchoueys, & some oys=
ters & musheroones if you h'aue them, then
set it ouer the fire & when the anchoueys
are Dissolued put in half a pound of butter,
& when it is mollted thicken the sauce with
the yolks of 2 Eggs beat with a little Vinager,
so you Dish being redy with sippess barberys
& Lemmon pour it of, & add some forceme=
at balls & sausages ~~oysters~~ & put in the midle a
Roasted foull or 4 Veal oliues —— —— ——

To make a Dish of Scotch Collops

take a large fillet of Veal & Cut of all the skin, then Cut the
Veal out in large thin Collops, & hack them with the back
of a large knife, & season them with salt nuttmeg some
Lemmonpile & thyme minced small, put on the yolks of 2 or
3 Eggs & mix them all up togather, & fry them in butter as
white as you Can, then pour out all most all the liquer & put
in half a pint of good beef gravey, a quarter of a pint of white
wine, 2 anchoveys, & some oyrsters & musheroones if you
have them, then set it ouer the fire & when the anchoveys are
Dissolved put in half a pound of buttcr, & when it is mellted
thicken the sauce with the yolks of 2 Eggs beat with a little
Vinager, so you Dish being redy with sippets barberys &
Lemmon pour it of, & add some forcemeat balls & sausages &
put in the midle a Roasted foull or 4 Veal olives

To Hash a Calues head (14)

first boyl the head tender & pull out all y̌ bones
then cut the meat in then slices, & put it
in to a stew pan or a frying pan with half
a pint of good beef gravey a quarter of a
pint of Clarrat some nutmeg some salt, half
a handfull of Capors & 2 anchoveys, half a
Lemon cut in bits & a little Vinager & some
oysters & mushrooms if you have them, then
set it over the fire, & when y̌ anchoveys are
Disolved put in half a pound of butter, &
when it is melted & your Dish redy as for
the Scotch Collops pour it of, & add some fryd bacon,
foreameatballs & if you please, sausages, put in y̌
midle a roasted foull or 4 veal olives — the brai
ns being parboyld cut them in slices & Dipp
them in the yolk of an Egge & fry them
brown to lay round the Dish

To Hash a Calves head

first boyl the head tendar & pull out all ye bones then Cut
the meat in thin slices & put it in to a stew pan or a frying
pan with half a pint of good beef gravey a quarter of a pint of
Clarrat some nuttmeg some salt, half a handfull of Capors & 2
anchoveys half a Lemon Cut in bits & a little Vinager & some
oyrsters & musheroones if you have them, then set it over the
fire, & when ye anchoveys are Dissolved put in half a pound of
butter, & when it is mellted & your Dish redy as for the Scotch
Collops pour it of, & add some fryd bacon, forcemeatballs &
if you please, sausages put in y^e midle a roasted foull or 4 veal
olives—the brains being parboyld Cut them in slices & Dipp
them in the yolk of an Egge & fry them brown to lay round
the Dish

To make Minct pyes

(15)

take of neats tongue or hart one pound & a
half. it being parboyld & blanched Chopp
it very small, then add to it 2 pound & a half
of good beef suet, add to it as many Currans,
one large nuttmeg, 3 penneyworth of Cloues
& as much mace beat fine, t 4 pippins
a little salt, half a pound of Raisins stoned
& Choped small, put in half a pint of sack
a little of the best brandey, a Quarter of a
paint of Zariuice, one pound of suger, a
little roasewatter tho rind of one large
Lemmon minced small, & put in the guice
ỹ you may put in of Candied orang Lemon
& Cittorn Each 2 ounces if you please

To make minct pyes

take of neats tongue or hart one pound & a half, it being
parboyld & blanched Chopp it very small, then add to it 2
pound & a half of good beef suet, add to it as many Currans
one large nuttmeg, 3 penneyworth of Cloves & as much mace
beat fine, 4 pippins a little salt, half a pound of Raisins stoned
& Choped small, put in half a pint of sack a little of the best
brandey, a quarter of a pint of Variuice, one pound of suger, a
little roasewatter the rind of one large Lemmon minced small,
& put in the juice y^n you may put in of Candied orang Lemon
& Cittorn Each 2 ounces if you please

To make a Good beef Graucy

(16)

take of 3 pound of lean beef ftakes & hack
them with the back of a Cleauor, & put it
in to a ftew pan or a frying pan with a
Quarter of a pound of Butter, ftrew in
fome falt. put in one fmall onion ftuk
Eliz with Cloues, put in fome whole popper,
Eliz: & mace & a fprigg of thyme, then Couer
it Down Cloafe & let it ftew ouer a foft
fire for allmoft half an chour or longer,
then put in a pint of watter or more
3 anchoueys, & a fmall piece of Lemmonpile
& Let it ftew fome fmall time longer.
then ftrain it of for ufe

To make a Good beef Gravey

take 3 pound of lean beef stakes & hack them with the back
of a Cleavor, & put it in to a Stew pan or a fryingpan with a
Quarter of a pound of butter, strew in some salt, put in one
small onion stuck with Cloves, put in some whole pepper, &
mace & a sprigg of thyme, then Cover it Down Cloase & let
it stew ouer a soft fire for allmost half an hour or longer, then
put in a pint of watter or more 3 anchoveys, & a small piece of
Lemmonpile & Let it stew some small time longer then strain
it of for use

(17)
To make London Wiggs

take 2 pound of the fineſt flour & rubb fine
in it half a pound of butter, half a pound
of fine ſuger, half an ounce of Canraway
ſeeds half a pint of aleyeſt, & 2 Eggs.
beat the Eggs yeſt a little of the flour &
3 or 4 ſpoonfulls of milk well togather
& ſtrain it in the midle of the flour, & ſtrew
ſome of the flour over it, & let it ſtand 12
hours or longer, then make it in a paiſt
prettey tendar, with luke warme milk, &
make them up, & ſet them by the fire one
hour or longer to riſe then waſh them over
with the yolk of one Egge beat with 2 ſpoon
fulls of milke

To make London wiggs

take 2 pound of the finest flour & rubb fine in it half a pound
of butter, half a pound of fine suger, half an ounce of Carraway
seeds half a pint of ale yest, & 2 Eggs. beat the Eggs yest a
little of the flour & 3 or 4 spoonfulls of milk well togather &
strain it in the midle of the flour, & strew some of the flour
over it, & let it stand 12 hours or longer then make it in a paist
prettey tendar, with luke warme milk, & make them up, & set
them by the fire one hour or longer to rise then wash them
ouer with the yolk of one Egge beat with 2 spoon fulls of milke

(15)

To make good forcemeat balls

take of Veal or poark half a pound & let it
be free from skin, y chop it very small,
& when you haue so Done add to it allmost
as much good beef suet as meat, & Chopp it
togather till y suet is fine y beat it in a
morter till it Cometh to a parfit paist,
then season it with pepper salt nuttmeg,
some Lemmonpile & thymd minced small
then worke it up with one or 2 Eggs as
you see good, & make it in little balls
the syse of a nuttmeg you may Colour
some of y green with spinedg if you please

To make good forcemeat balls

take of Veal or poark half a pound & let it be free from skin, y^n
Chop it very small, & when you have so Done add to it allmost
as much good beef suet as meat, & Chopp it togather till y^e
suet is fine y^n beat it in a morter till it Cometh to a parfit paist,
then season it with pepper salt nuttmeg, some Lemmonpile &
thyme minced small, then worke it up with one or 2 Eggs as
you see good, & make it in little balls the syse of a nuttmeg you
may Colour some of y^m green with spinedg if you please

(19)

To make a Dish of newcolich puding

take y crumb of 4 penney loues grated & add to it one pound of ~~~~ good beef suet shrad small, put to it as may currans, some nuttmeg, a little salt, 4 ounces of fine suger. 5 Eggs beat with a little sack or brandy, you may put in a little Roosewatter if you please, & what Cream will temper it in a prettey stiff paist, to make it in little pudding in the sheap of an Egge but longer, & this Quantity will make a Dozen & a half & fry them with half a pound of butter, & Dish them out with a quaking puding in the midle, then pour ouer some butter & strew ouer some fine suger, — — — — — — — ♥

To make a Quaking puding

take 2 penney loaues y Crust being cut of, cut the bread in thin slices, & put it in to a bacon or pan with what boyling milk well wett it or more & w[hen] it is allmost cold put in 6 Eggs well beat with a little of the best brandy & a little roaskwatter if you please, put to it 2 ounces of fine suger, a little salt & nuttmeg, so tye it up in a bagg & boyl it one hour _____

To make a Dish of newcolidg puddings

take y^e Crumb of 4 penney loves grated, & add to it one pound
of good beef suet, shrad small, put to it as may Currans, some
nuttmeg, a little salt, 4 ounces of fine suger, 5 Eggs beat with
a little sack or brandy, you may put in a little Roasewatter if
you please, & what Cream will temper it in a prettey stiff
paist, so make it in little pudding in the sheap of an Egge
but longer, & this quantity will make a Dozen & a half &
fry them with half a pound of butter, & Dish them out with
a quaking puding in the midle, then pour ouer some butter
& strew over some fine suger

To make a quaking puding

take 2 penney loaves ye Crust being Cut of, Cut the bread
in thin slices, & put it in to a bacon or pan with what boyling
milk well wett it or more & w^n it is allmost Cold put in 6 Eggs
well beat with a little of the best brandy & a little roasewatter
if you please, put to it 2 ounces of fine suger, a little salt &
nuttmeg, so tye it up in a bagg & boyl it one hour

(20)

To make Ayres his pancakes

beat 8 Eggs with a little of the best brandey, &
3 Quarters of a pound of the finest flour, put in
a little nuttmeg, a little salt, & half a pound
of butter melted in a pint of Cream, or milk
& when it is allmost Cold mix it all togather
with 2 ounces of fine Suger, & fry them in
a Dry pan without any fatt, & let the pan
be hot when you begin, & fry them only of
one side, & strew some fine suger between
Every pancke as you put them in the Dish,
& w'n they are all fryd turn them upside Down
in another Dish that the brown side may be
upward, & strew over some fine Suger ——

To make Ayres his pancakes

beat 8 Eggs with a little of the best brandey, & 3 Quarters of
a pound of the finest flour, put in a little nuttmeg, a little salt,
& half a pound of butter mellted in a pint of Cream, or milk
& when it is allmost Cold mix it all togather with 2 ounces of
fine suger, & fry them in a Dry pan without any fatt, & let the
pan be hot when you begin, & fry them only of one side, &
Strew some fine suger between Every pancake as you put them
in the Dish, and w[n] they are all fryd turn them upside Down in
another Dish that the brown side may be upward, & strew over
some fine suger

To Pott a Hare

(21)

Cut the hair in 4 or 5 pieces & take it tendar
in watter, then take all the meat from the
bones & pick out all the skin, then beat the
meat in a Cloth with a rouling pin to Drink
up the watter, then beat it fine in a morter
& season it with half a nuttmeg some salt
as you see good. a Quarter of an ounce of pepper
& a penneyworth of Cloues & machen
mixe it up in a paist with Clarreyfied butter
as you Do the poted beef, then press it Cloase
in your pot & pour some butter ouer it

To make paist for paskeys or meat pyes in Dishes

allow to a pound of flour half a pound of butter
& one Egge Deuide the butter in 3 parts brake in
one & roul in the rest all twice

To Pott a Hare

Cut the hair in 4 or 5 pieces & bake it tendar in watter, then
take all the meat from the bones & pick out all the skin, then
beat the meat in a Cloth with a rouling pin to Drink up the
watter, then beat it fine in a morter & season it with half a
nuttmeg some salt as you see good a quarter of an ounce of
pepper & a penneyworth of Cloves & mace then mix it up in
a paist with Clarreyfied butter as you Do the poted beef, then
press it Cloase in your pot & pour some butter over it

To make paist for pasteys or meat pyes in Dishes

allow to a pound of flour half a pound of butter & one Egge
Devide the butter in 3 parts brake in one & roul in the rest att
twice

To Make Cheescakes

take the Curd of 8 Quarts of milk which is run
not to hot or to Cold & Dry it well in a Cloth,
then worke in it 3 Quartens of a pound of butter,
3 grated biskets or as much bread, a little salt, a
little Clouef mace & nuttmeg, 10 Eggs well beat
with a little of the best brandey, you may put
in a little roasewatter if you please & Leaue
out 5 whites, & a pint of good Cream, put in
about 3 Quarters of a pound of fine suger. y
work it through a Coars hair siue, & then the
put in one pound of Currans well washed &
Dryd so the Coffins being hooped fill them you
may put in half a pound of almonds blanched
& beat fine with a little Roasewatter if you
please

To Make Cheescakes

take the Curd of 8 quarts of milk which is run not to hot or to
Cold & Dry it well in a Cloth, then worke in it 3 quarters of a
pound of butter, 3 grated biskets or as much bread, a little salt,
a little Cloves mace & nuttmeg, 10 Eggs well beat with a little
of the best brandey, you may put in a little roasewatter if you
please & Leave out 5 whites, & a pint of good Cream put in
a bout 3 quarters of a pound of fine suger, y^n work it through
a Coars hair sive, & then put in one pound of Currans well
washed & Dryd so the Coffins being hooped fill them you may
put in half a pound of almonds blanched & beat fine with a
little Roasewatter if you please

To presarue Damsons for Sweet me- a/s

take y largest Damsons you can get & with a pen
knife Cut them Down one side only the out skin
then take their waight in Double refined suger
& put ite in to a presaruing pan with what
watter will wett it or more so boyl it up
& Clarrey fie it with the white of an Egge &
skim it Clean of, then set y Syrop by till
Lukewarme, then put in your Damsons & set y
by for 3 or 4 Dayes heating them up allmost scalding
hot Every Day then quit let them boyl up &
put them in glassees & boyl the Syrop to a
Conuenant thickness & pour to them; — — —

To Presarue Damsons for tarts

put them in to an Earthen pot & set them in a
slack ouin till y skin begineth to Crack then
take out the pot & allow to Every Quart half a
pound of suger, & lay the suglr all ouer them &
pour ouer the suger before it is Dissolued a Cake
of mutton fat & tye y Down ——

To presarve Damsons for sweet meats

take ye largest Damsons you can get & with a pen knife Cut them Down one side only the out skin then take their waight in Doublerefined suger, & put it in to a presaruing pan with what watter will wett it or more so boyl it up & Clarreyfie it with the white of an Egge & skim it Clean of, then set ye syrop by till Lukewarme, then put in your Damsons & set y^m by for 3 or 4 Dayes heating them up allmost scalding hot Euery Day then just let them boyl up & put them in glassees & boyl the syrop to a Convenant thickness & pour to them

To Presarve Damsons for tarts

put them in to an Earthen pot & set them in a slack ovin till the skin begineth to Crack, then take out the pot & allow to Every quart half a pound of suger, & lay the suger all over them & pour over the suger before it is Dissolved a Cake of mutton fat and tye y^m Down

To Pickle Musheroones

let y^m be but of one nights groth & throw them
in watter, & wash them Clean with a bitt of
flannill & Cut of the stools, then throw the
musheroones in boyling watter will what watter
milk will Colour the watter white, & a little salt,
& let them boyl about a Quarter of an
hour then take y^m out & Dry them on a
Cloth & t put them in to half watter &
half vinager for 2 or 3 Dayes, then Dry y^m
as before & put them in to half white
wine & half white wine vinager put in
some whole pepper, race ginger some mace
a little salt, 2 or 3 bayleaues & a piece of Lemon
pile, then pour over a Cak of mutton fatt &
stye them Down

To Pickle Musheroones

let y^m be but of one nights groth & throw them in watter &
wash them Clean with a bitt of flannill, & Cut of the roots,
then throw the musheroones in boyling watter with what milk
will Colour the watter white, & a little salt, & let them boyl
a bout a quarter of an hour then take y^m out & Dry them on
a Cloth & put them in to half watter & half vinager for 2 or
3 Dayes, then Dry y^m as before & put them ito half white
wine & half white wine vinager put in some whole pepper,
raceginger some mace a little salt, 2 or 3 bayleaves & a piece of
Lemonpile, then pour over a Cak of mutton fatt & tye them
Down

To Pickle Cucumbars (25)

take ye midle fize Cucumbars & put them into
a Deep Earthen pot with 3 or 4 topps of Dill,
yⁿ boyl your pickle & pour to them boyling
hot 3 or 4 times once Every Day & keep them
Cloase Courd that no fteam may Come out, —
make your pickle with ye beft white wineuinagier
raceginger whole pepper, & half a handfull of
falt allow to 2 hundred half an ounce of —
pepper, & as much ginger, then if they are
not fo green as you would haue y^m put them
in to a bellmetle or brafs pot & paift Down
the Lidd all round that no fteam may Come out,
& fet them ouer a uery foft fire guft to
keep hot till they are as green as you would
haue them, then pour them out & Couer y^m
Down Cloafe

To Pickle Cucumbars

take ye midle size Cucumbars & put them in to a Deep
Earthen pot with 3 or 4 topps of Dill, y^n boyl your pickl &
pour to them boyling hot 3 or 4 times once Every Day & keep
them Cloase Covrd that no steam may come out, make your
pickle with ye best white wine vinager raceginger whole pepper,
& half a handfull of salt allow to 2 hundred half an ounce of
pepper, & as much ginger, then if they are not so green as you
would haue y^m put them into a bellmetle or brass pot & paist
Down the lidd all round that no steam may Come out, & set
them over a very soft fire just to keep hot till they are as green
as you would have them, then pour them out & Cover y^m
Down Cloase

To make Ginger Bread

(26)

take 2 pound & a half of fine flour, & add to
it half a pound of brown suger, & 2 Eggs, then
take of Carraway seeds, Coliander seeds, & racl ging
Er Each one ounce beat the Coliander seeds &
ginger & sift it to your flour, then melt
half a pound of butter in a pound of treacle
& pour it to your flour when Lukewarme
& make it in a paist with 2 ounces of Candie
orang pile Cut in bitts, then make it in Cakes
of what size you please, & when they are baked
Dipp them in boyling watter & ale to glaze
them

To Pickle kidney beans

let them be the Dwalf beans for this use if possable, & boyl up what whit wine vinager you think
will Cover them, & some salt, & pour it to them
boyling hot & Cover them Down Cloas, & the next
Day green them as you Do the Cucumbers

To make Ginger Bread

take 2 pound & a half of fine flour, & add to it half a pound
of brown suger, & 2 Eggs, then take of Carraway seeds,
Colianderseeds & raceginger Each one ounce beat the
Colianderseeds & Ginger & sift it to your flour, then mellt
half a pound of butter in a pound of treacle & pour it to your
flour when Lukewarme & make it in a paist with 2 ounces of
Candied orang pile Cut in bitts, then make it in cakes of what
size you please, & when they are baked Dipp them in boyling
watter & ale to glaze them

To Pickle kidney beans

let them be the Dwalf beans for this use if possable, & boyl
up what white wine vinager you think will Cover them, &
some salt & pour it to them boyling hot & Cover them Down
Cloase, & the next Day green them as you Do the Cucumbars

(27)

To make a marmalid of Quinces or pippins

first pair & boyl them very tendar ij scrape
all the pulp from the Coarr & put it in a skillat
with the same waight in Double refined suger,
& boyl it togather keeping it stirring till it
will Cleave from the bottom, then put in a
little scuttchan Ell beat fine, & let it boyle
some time longer, as you see it of a good red,
then put it up for use — — — —

To make a Jam of Rasberyes

take a pint of ij largest ras̃ps, & pulp 3 parts
of ym through a Cears hair sive & then put the
pulp & the whole rasberyes in to a skillat with
half a pound of Double refined suger & boyl it
over a Cleer fire keeping it stirring till it is
some what stiff, & the syrop wasted then put it
in Glasses

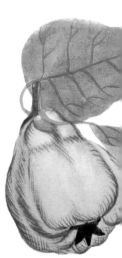

To make a marmalid of Quinces or pippins

first pair & boyl them very tendar y^n scrape all the pulp
from the Coarr & put it in a skillat with the same waight in
Doublerefined Suger, & boyl it togather keeping it stirring till
it will Cleave from the bottom, then put in a little scuttch an
Eell beat fine, & let it boyle some time longer, as you see it of a
good red, then put it up for use

To make a Jam of Rasberyes

take a pint of ye largest rasps, & pulp 3 parts of y^m through a
Coars hair fine & then put the pulp & the whole rasberyes in
to a skillat with half a pound of Doublerefined suger, & boyl it
over a Cleer fire keeping it stirring till it is some what stiff, &
the Syrop wasted then put it in Glasses

To make a Cabage Puding (28)

take 3 Quarters of a pound of good beef suet or
marrow & shread it very fine, & add to it as
many Currans & as much suger. then your
Dish beeing Garnished with puff paist take 2
penny loaues, the Crust being Cut of Cut the
bread in thin slices, then put all ouer the
bottom a laying of Currans suet & suger, &
then a laying of bread, so put a laying of one
& a laying of the other till you haue filld
the Dish, then beat 5 or 6 Eggs with a little
of the best brandey, & then mixe with them
a pint & a half of Cream with a little nutt
meg & pour it in your Dish then you may
Cut out a flurantine pattorn for the lidd or
you may bake it without,

To make a Cabage Puding

take 3 quarters of a pound of good beef suet or marrow &
shrad it very fine, & add to it as many Currans & as much
suger, then your Dish being Garnished with puff paist take 2
penney loaves, the Crust being Cut of Cut the bread in thin
slices, then put all over the bottom a laying of Currans suet
& suger, & then a laying of bread, so put a laying of one & a
laying of the other till you have filld the Dish, then beat 5 or 6
Eggs with a little of the best brandey, & then mix with them a
pint & a half of Cream with a little nuttmeg & pour it in your
Dish then you may Cut out a flurantine pattern for the lidd or
you may bake it without

(29)

To make a millet seed puding

take half a pound of seed & boyl it in milk
till it is very tendar & thick & when it is
cold add to itt haef a pound of batter broke in
small bitts, put to it haef a pound off fine
suger, haef a pound of Currans, if you pleaß,
a little salt, a little nuttmeg, 3 grated bisketes or
bread, 5 Eggs beat with a little brandy, you
may put in one ounce of Cittorn & as much
lemmon if you pleaß, & bake it in puffpaist
as you Do the Lemon or orang puding ——

To make a Jelly of Rasberyes

take the quice of one Quart of Currance, & ye quice
of one pint of rasberyes & put it in to a skillat
with one pound of Double refined suger, &
boyl it till you think it will Jelly keeping it
skiming, then put it in Glasses

To make a millet seed puding

take half a pound of seed & boyl it in milk till it is very tendar
& thick & when it is Cold add to it half a pound of butter
broke in small bitts, put to it half a pound of fine suger, half a
pound of Currans, if you please, a little salt, a little nuttmeg, 3
grated bisketes or bread, 5 Eggs beat with a little brandy, you
may put in one ounce of Cittorn & as much Lemmon if you
please, & bake it in puffpaist as you Do the Lemon or orang
puding

To make a Jelly of Rasberyes

take the juice of one quart of Currance, & ye juice of one
pint of rasberyes & put it in to a skillat with one pound
of Doublerefined suger, & boyl it till you think it will jelly
keeping it skiming, then put it in Glasses

To make a (30) Rich Seed Cake

rub one pound of butter fine in one pound of
y finest flour put to it one pound of single
fined suger, sifted, 2 ounces of Carraway seeds
12 newlaid Eggs well beat with 4 spoonfulls
of y best brandy, & leave out 6 whites, then work
it with your hands for half an hour or longer,
then the ouin being redy, bake it in a tin puding
pan well butterd, bake it 3 hours in not to rash
an ouin put in 2 penney worth of Cloues & mace,

To make Ayres His puding

ake one pound af good beef suet & shread it very
fine then add to it, one pound of raisins stoned
& chopped but not to small, 7 Eggs beat with
a little brandy put in a little saet & nuttmeg
3 large spoonfulls of the finest flour & 3 of fine
suger, y mix it well togather tye it up in a bagg
& boyl it 4 hours then pour ouer some butter &
strew ouer some fine suger — — — —

To make a Rich Seed Cake

rub one pound of butter fine in one pound of ye finest flour
put to it one pound of singlerefined suger, sifted, 2 ounces of
Carraway seeds 12 newlaid Eggs well beat with 4 spoon fulls of
ye best brandy, & Leave out 6 whites, then work it with your
hands for half an hour or longer, then the ovin being redy bake
it in a tin puding pan well butterd, bake it 3 hours in not to
rash an ovin put in 2 penneyworth of Cloves & mace

To make Ayres His puding

take one pound of good beef suet, & shrad it very fine, then
add to it, one pound of raisins stoned & Chopped but not
to small, 5 Eggs beat with a little brandy put in a little salt &
nuttmeg 3 large spoonfulls of the finest flour & 3 of fine suger,
y^n mix it well togather tye it up in a bagg & boyl it 4 hours
then pour over some butter & strew over some fine suger

(82)
To fricacie a couple of Rabits, or 3 large Chickens

Cut them in pieces but not to large & season ym
with salt, nuttmeg some parsley thyme & lemon
pile minced small, then fry it with half a pint
of stall beer & a pint of watter till it is
throughly Done, then pour out allmost all ye
liquer & put in half a pint of good beef
gravey a quarter of a pint of Clarret, 2 anchoueys
& some oysters & musheroones if you have ym
so set it over the fire & when the anchoueys are
Disolved put in half a pound of butter, & when
it is melted thicken the sauce with the yolks of 2
eggs beat with a little vinager, so your Dish being
redy with sippets, barberyes & Lemon pour it of
you may add some fryd bacon forcemeatballs &
if you please sausages, put in the middle a if
foulls skin them first.

To fricacie a couple of Rabits, or 3 large Chickens

Cut them in pieces but not to large & season y^m with salt,
nuttmeg some parsley thyme & lemon pile minced small, then
fry it with half a pint of stall [small] beer & a pint of watter till
it is throughly Done, then pour out allmost all ye liquer & put
in half a pint of good beef gravey a quarter of a pint of Clarret,
2 anchoveys & some oyrsters & musheroones if you haue y^m
so set it over the fire & when the anchoveys are Dissolved put
in half a pound of butter, & when it is mellted thicken the
sauce with the yolks of 2 Eggs beat with a little vinager, so your
Dish being redy with sippets, barberyes & Lemon pour it of
you may add some fryd bacon forcemeatballs & if you please
sausages, if foulls skin them first

(33)

To Make Queen Cakes

take one pound of flour
one pound of butter
one pound of fine suger,
one pound of Currans
3 pennyworth of Cloues & mace beat fine,
10 new laid Eggs well beat with 4 spoonfulls.
of the best brandey & leaue out 8 whites,
then worke it with your hands for half an
hour or Longer, then thee pans being butterd
& the ouin redy fill them & scrape ouer
some Doubbrefined suger, you may put in of
Candied Lemmon & Cittorn Each one ounce
if you please,

To Make Queen Cakes

take one pound of flour
one pound of butter
one pound of fine suger,
one pound of Currans

3 penneyworth of Cloves & mace beat fine, 10 new laid Eggs
well beat with 4 spoonfulls of the best brandey & leave out
8 whites, then worke it with your hands for half an hour or
longer, then thee pans being butterd & the ovin redy fill them
& scrape over some Doublerefined suger, you may put in of
Candied Lemmon & Cittorn Each one ounce if you please

(34)

To Collcr a Parkers head

First boyle the Cheeks tendar then pull out all the
bones, & seasson the Cheeks with a good Deal of
salt, then lay the thin End of one Cheek to the
thick End of the other with the tongue in the
midle & roul them up in a Cloth & tye the
Cloth at Each End of the Coller, then bind hard
all round on the Cloth to Close the Coller you
6 yards of Coars tape, & when it is Cold take of
the Cloth & then put the Coller in souce Drink

To make Lemmon or orang tarts

make the Coffines as you Do the tartletts, & make
the filling as you Do the Lemmon or orang pud
ing add to more biskets To make it stiffer —

To Coller a Poarkers head

first boyle the Cheeks tendar then pull out all the bones, & season the Cheeks with a good Deal of salt, then lay the thin End of one Cheek to the thick End of the other with the tongue in the midle & roul them up in a Cloth & and tye the Cloth at Each End of the Coller, then bind hard all round on the Cloth to Cloase the Coller 5 or 6 yards of Coars tape, & when it is Cold take of the Cloth & then put the Coller in souce Drink

To make Lemmon or orang tarts

make the Coffines as you Do the tartlitts, & make the filling as you Do the Lemmon or orang puding add to more biskets to make it Stiffer

(35)

To make a Dish of Veal oliues

Take a large fillet of veal & Cut it out in
large thin Collops a bout 5 or 6 inches long & as
broad as well you Can, & season them as you Do y
scotch Collops, then lay on euery Collop a thin
slice of fat bacon, of y same proportion, & roul
them up in little rollers & spitt them on long skurs
y Crass way as you Do larks, & Lard them with bacon
& tye them to a spitt, & roast them, then Dish them
out with a roasted foull in the midle & make
the sauce as for the forced lamb or mitton adding
more butter & make the sauce thicker you may
add some forcemeat balls sausages oyrsters & mushe
roomes if you haue them,

To make a Dish of Veal Cuttlets

t y veal out as for y oliues, & season them the same
lard them th bacon & fry them in butter as white
you Can, then Dish them out with a roasted foull
the midle & make the sauce as for the oliues, &
d some forcemeat balls sausages oysters & musherooms
f you haue them

To make a dish of Veal olives

take a large fillet of veal & Cut it out in large thin Collops a
bout 5 or 6 inches long & as broad as well you can, & season
them as you Do ye Scotch Collops, then lay on Every Collop
a thin slice of fat bacon, of ye same proportion, & roul them
up in little Collers & spitt them on long squrs ye Crass way as
you Do larks, & lard them with bacon & tye them to a spitt,
& roast them, then Dish them out with a roasted foull in the
midle & make the sauce for the forced lamb or mutton adding
more butter & make the sauce thicker you may add some
forcemeat balls sausages oyrsters & musheroones if you have
them

To make a Dish of Veal Cuttlets

cut ye veal out as for ye olives, & season them the same lard
them wth bacon & fry them in butter as white as you can, then
Dish them out with a roasted foull in the midle & make the
sauce as for the oliues, & add some forcemeatballs sausages
oyrsters & musheroones if you have them

To make a Dish of good brown Sup

(36)

Take a large Leg of beef & Cut it in 2 or 3 pieces &
boyl it in a Conuenant Quantity of watter
all to mash, then strain of the liquer in to a
stewpan or pot which must be no more y̅ a bout
2 Quarts, & take of the fatt, then put in a Quart
of good grauey, thicken it as you please with
grated bread, put in some salt, half a pint of
forcemeatballs the size of a nuttmeg, put in some
parsley & thyme minced small, & let it boyl till
the balls are Done then pour it in your supe
Dish with a boyld foull in the midle & put in a
penney loafe Cut like Dyes & fryd brown in butter

To hash a neats tongue, not salted

First boyl the tongue tendar & blanch im & Cut of
the root then Cut the tongue in uery thin slices &
put it in to a stewpan or a frying pan & Do it
the same way as you Do the Calues head hash with
a roasted foull in y̅ midle or 4 ueal oliues

To make a Disk of good bronn sup

take a large leg of beef & Cut it in 2 or 3 pieces & boyl it in a
Convenant quantity of watter all to mash, then strain of the
liquer in to a stewpan or pot which must be no more y^n a bout
2 quarts, & take of the fatt, then put in a quart of good gravey,
thicken it as you please with grated bread, put in some salt,
half a pint of forcemeatballs the size of a nuttmeg, put in some
parsley and thyme minced small, & let it boyl till the balls are
Done then pour it in your supe Dish with a boyld foull in the
midle & put in a penney loafe Cut like Dyes & fryd brown in
butter

To hash a neats tongue, not salted

first boyl the tongue tendar & blanch im & Cut of the root
then Cut the tongue in very thin slices & put it in to a stew
pan or a frying pan & Do it the same way as you Do the
Calves head hash with a roasted foull in ye midle or 4 veal
olives

(37)

To force a Leg of Lamb or mutton

First Cut a long hole in the fleshy part of the
Leg & take out half a pound of the Lean & make
forcemeat of it, as you Do the other force meat,
put it in again & sow, ys the place you Cut
& Lard the Leg ouer with bacon & roast it, &
make the sauce with allmost half a pint of
good beef graueys a: Little Clarret & anchoueys
a small pice of butter, if you please, & some
oyisters & musherooues if you haue them———

To make a Goosbery flurantine

take 2 Quarts of goosberys & bake them red with one
pound of suger, then make them in puffpaist as
you Do the Lemmon or orang puding but you must
not marsh them

To force a Leg of Lamb or mutton

first Cut a long hole in the fleshy part of the leg & take out half a pound
of the lean & make a forcemeat of it, as you Do the other forcemeat, then
put it in a gain & sow up the place you Cut & lard the leg over with bacon
& roast it, & make the sauce with allmost half a pint of good beef gravey,
a little Clarret 2 anchoveys a small piece of butter if you please, & some
oyrsters & musheroones if you have them

To make a Goosbery flurantine

take 2 quarts of goossberys & bake them red with one pound of suger,
then make them in puffpaist as you Do the lemmon or orang puding but
you must not marsh them

Glossary

aleyest ale yeast, the live yeast used in brewing

at each hand at both ends

barberyes, barbarys sharp-flavoured red berries from a common shrub of the berberis variety.

Bath cakes small cakes to be served with wine, coffee or beer

bell-metle bell metal, the bronze used in bell-making, or an alloy similar to it. The attractive idea that mortars, skillets, etc. were made from the left-overs from bell-casting is probably not true because a more valuable high-tin bronze was used in the church bells, but such culinary objects were often made by bell-casters. During the Commonwealth, when it was forbidden to ring church bells, many bell-makers had to find alternate outlets for their skills and in the Oxford area a family called Neale of Burford became especially prominent (*Mortars Made by the Neale Family of Bronze Founders*, Ashmolean Museum exhibition catalogue, 1996). Bell metal and brass were valued in the kitchen and at table because they were low conductors of heat and did not easily crack. The handles would remain cool, and the vessels could be used for substances with high boiling-points such as sugar (Rachel Feilden, *Irons in the Fire*, pp. 76-7). The founder of New College, William of Wickham, had ordained in the fiftieth clause of his statutes that brass and pewter plate should be kept on the ground floor of the muniment tower (Information from Mrs. Caroline Dalton). Bell-metal and brass would probably have 'restored' the green colour to pickled cucumbers and beans, as Ayres claims, through chemical reactions which it would be undesirable to repeat in modern kitchens.

bronn supe brown soup

cabage puding probably so called because the custard mixture covering it would form a wrinkled skin like the leaves of a cabage. Rachel Feild notes a dish called 'cabbage cream', formed by skimming the skin from the cream and building it up in layers with sugar and rosewater sprinkled between the leaves (*Irons in the Fire*, p.145).

cittorn citron, the fruit of *citrus medica*, larger, less acid and with a thicker rind than lemon. Citron-water may have been brandy flavoured with citron or lemon (*Shorter Oxford Dictionary*, 1974).

coffins pastry cases

collard collared, formed into a ring, often served with a roast placed in the centre - a popular method of presentation for a festive dish

collop slice or piece of meat

double/dubble refined sugar white sugar, which had been through an extra refining process. 'Single refined sugar' would have been brown. The secondary refining processes were often carried out in the country of import, as the cargo was likely to be contaminated with sea-water after the long voyage from the West Indies. See also p10 of Introduction.

dyes cut like dyes, diced

florantine, flurandine shallow round pie made with very thin pastry, often with a cut-out decoration on the top part

forcemeat stuffing

hoop cake-tin

hudd hulls, outer casing

lard (verb) to thread strips of fat or fatty bacon through meat in order to keep it moist during cooking

live liver

maligoes raisins (from Malaga)

neat bovine animal such as ox or cow

ovin oven

papord papered

penny loaf a plain penny loaf was made with coarse flour and weighed about 12 ozs - 1 lb, 400-500 gms. A penny white loaf was half that size but of better quality, made with milk, flour and eggs (Elizabeth David, *English Bread and Yeast Cookery*, 1977, pp. 339-40).

pippin apple, especially dessert variety

quart two pints, a little over a litre

raceginger root ginger

Radolphus Ralph

rand cut or slice of meat

rash [of heat] extreme heat

sack fortified white wine esp. sherry

salt petter saltpetre, used in preserving. It gave a good red colour. The Prospect Books edition (1983) of Hannah Glasse's cookery book has a comprehensive note on the subject, p. 197.

scotch [verb] gash, score, as in Shakespeare's 'We have scotched the snake, not killed it' (*Macbeth*, act 3, sc.2, l.11)

setlins Settlings, dregs

sippets small triangles of bread, fried, toasted or dried beside a fire till crisp

sivel Seville

skillet long-handled cooking vessel resembling a frying-pan but deeper and with three legs. It could be placed directly on to the hearth.

small beer home-brewed ale very weak in alcohol, commonly drunk at breakfast and by children because water was often unsafe. It usually contained cottage-garden or rural flavourings such as herbs, nettles and heather, not hops. My grandmother in South Wales brewed a small ale which she called 'herb beer', flavoured with nettles, until the 1950s. It was greyish in colour, rather sweet, and said to 'clear the blood'. She was from a rigidly teetotal Methodist family, but this was considered a perfectly acceptable drink.

souce souse, to pickle or steep in brine or vinegar

varjuice, verjuice acid juice of sour or unripe fruit. Lemon juice, unsweetened grape juice or wine vinegar would be modern substitutes.

wiggs a Lent speciality, small cakes or loaves, originally made from a round cake cut into wedges. Ayres' 'London' recipe may have been considered a metropolitan sophistication, but William Ellis gives a very plain version for farm use, which was served hot when the men came in from harvesting and dipped in ale for supper (*Country Housewife's Family Companion*, ed. Malcolm Thick (London: Prospect Books, 2000), p.125).

SELECT BIBLIOGRAPHY

Aylmer, Ursula, ed., *Oxford Food, an Anthology* (Oxford: Ashmolean Museum & Bodleian Library, 1995).

Ayres, Ralph, *A Little Book of Recipes of New College two hundred years ago*, ed. L.G. Wickham Legg (Oxford: Oxford University Press, 1922).

Buxton, John, and Penry Williams, *New College, Oxford, 1379-1979* (New College, Oxford, 1979).

Davidson, Alan, *The Oxford Companion to Food* (Oxford: Oxford University Press, 1999).

Feild, Rachel, *Irons in the Fire: a history of cooking equipment* (Marlborough: Crowood Press, 1984).

Glasse, Hannah, *The Art of Cookery made Plain and Easy* [facsimile of 1747 edn.]. (London: Prospect Books, 1983).

Hearne, Thomas, *The Remains*, ed. John Buchanan-Brown (London and Fontwell: Centaur Press, 1966).

History of the University of Oxford, Vol. V, The Eighteenth Century, ed. L.S. Sutherland and L.G. Mitchell (Oxford: Clarendon Press, 1986).

Kidder, Edward, *E. Kidder's Receipts of Pastry and Cooking for the Use of his Scholars* [facsimile edn.], introduced by Jane Jakeman (Oxford: Ashmolean Museum, 2001).

Midgley, Graham, *University Life in Eighteenth-Century Oxford* (New Haven and London: Yale University Press, 1996).

Quayle, Eric, *Old Cookery Books, An Illustrated History* (London: Studio Vista, 1978).

Smith, A. H., *New College, Oxford and its buildings* (Oxford: Oxford University Press, 1952).

Index of Recipies

Numbers refer to the pages of the transcribed recipes. The spelling has occasionally been modernized for clarity.